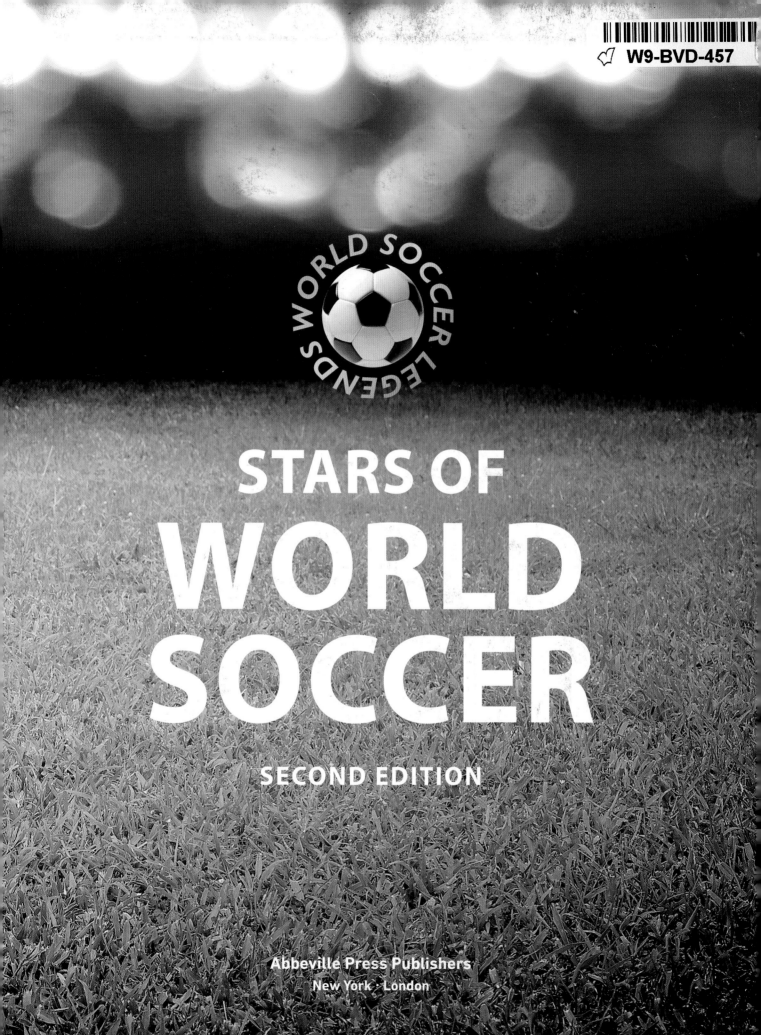

WORLD SOCCER LEGENDS

STARS OF WORLD SOCCER

SECOND EDITION

Abbeville Press Publishers

New York · London

A portion of this book's proceeds are donated to the **Hugo Bustamante AYSO Playership Fund**, a national scholarship program to help ensure that no child misses the chance to play AYSO Soccer. Donations to the fund cover the cost of registration and a uniform for a child in need.

Text by Illugi Jökulsson
Design and layout: Árni Torfason

For the English-language edition
Project Editor: Sharon Lucas
Proofreader: Ashley Benning
Composition: Ada Rodriguez
Production manager: Louise Kurtz

PHOTOGRAPHY CREDITS

Getty Images: pp. 18–19 (Chris Brunskill Ltd), p. 36 and front cover top left (Robbie Jay Barratt–AMA)

Shutterstock: pp. 6–7 (kivnl), pp. 8–9 and back cover center (Marcos Mesa Sam Wordley), pp. 10–11 (Dziurek), pp. 13 (Thiago Dias Rodrigues), pp. 14–15 (kivnl), pp. 16–17 (Marco Iacobucci EPP), pp. 20–21 (Vlad1988), pp. 22–23 (mooinblack), pp. 24 (A.PAES), pp. 26–27 (Maxisport), p. 29 and back cover bottom (CosminIftode), pp. 30–31 and front cover bottom right (Ververidis Vasilis), pp. 32–33 (Christian Bertrand), pp. 34–35 (daykung), p. 38 and front cover top center (Maxisport), pp. 40–41 (EFECREATA.COM), pp. 42–43 (CosminIftode), pp. 44–45 and back cover top (AGIF), p. 46 (Maxisport), pp. 48–49 (Ververidis Vasilis), p. 50 (CosminIftode), pp. 54–55 (Marco Iacobucci EPP), pp. 56–57 (CP DC Press), pp. 58–59 (CosminIftode), pp. 60–61 (Maxisport), front cover top right (CP DC Press), front cover bottom left (Christian Bertrand)

Árni Torfason: pp. 52–53

First published in the United States of America in 2018 by Abbeville Press, 116 West 23rd Street, New York NY 10011

Second Edition
10 9 8 7 6 5 4 3 2 1

ISBN 978-0-7892-1316-7

Library of Congress Cataloguing-in-Publication Data available upon request

For bulk and premium sales and for text adoption procedures, write to Customer Service Manager, Abbeville Press, 116 West 23rd Street, New York, NY 10011, or call 1-800-ARTBOOK.

Visit Abbeville Press online at www.abbeville.com.

CONTENTS

For the past few years, Sergio Agüero has been one of soccer's most reliable strikers. It doesn't matter what goes on at Manchester City—Agüero will deliver his 20 to 30 goals a season regardless. He will always be adored in the blue part of Manchester for his feat in his first season at the club, 2011–2012. In the last game, Agüero scored in added time, in the 94th minute, with the last kick of the game against Queens Park Rangers. This was the goal that gave Manchester City its first Premier League title in 44 years, taking it away from rivals Manchester United. It was an unbelievable moment—one that will live forever in the history of Mancunian soccer.

Agüero has scored all kinds of goals, but he tends to be at his best when he can use his explosive pace to go past defenders inside the penalty area. He's not the tallest of players, but he's strong as an ox and technically gifted. He has already become City's top scorer, and manager Guardiola seems to appreciate having this firecracker within his ranks.

Looking at Agüero's career, the only disappointment is his being a runner-up at the big tournaments, despite having been so close to winning a number of times. He was not at his best when Argentina faced Germany in the 2014 World Cup final in Brazil, where he and his teammate Messi had to accept defeat.

AGÜERO

Agüero played his first game in the Argentinian league for Independiente in 2003, having just turned 15, breaking the record held by Diego Maradona, who until then had been the youngest player in the league. It's a fun coincidence that Agüero later married Maradona's daughter, Giannina. They got divorced, but have a son named Benjamín. With those genes, he will probably go places!

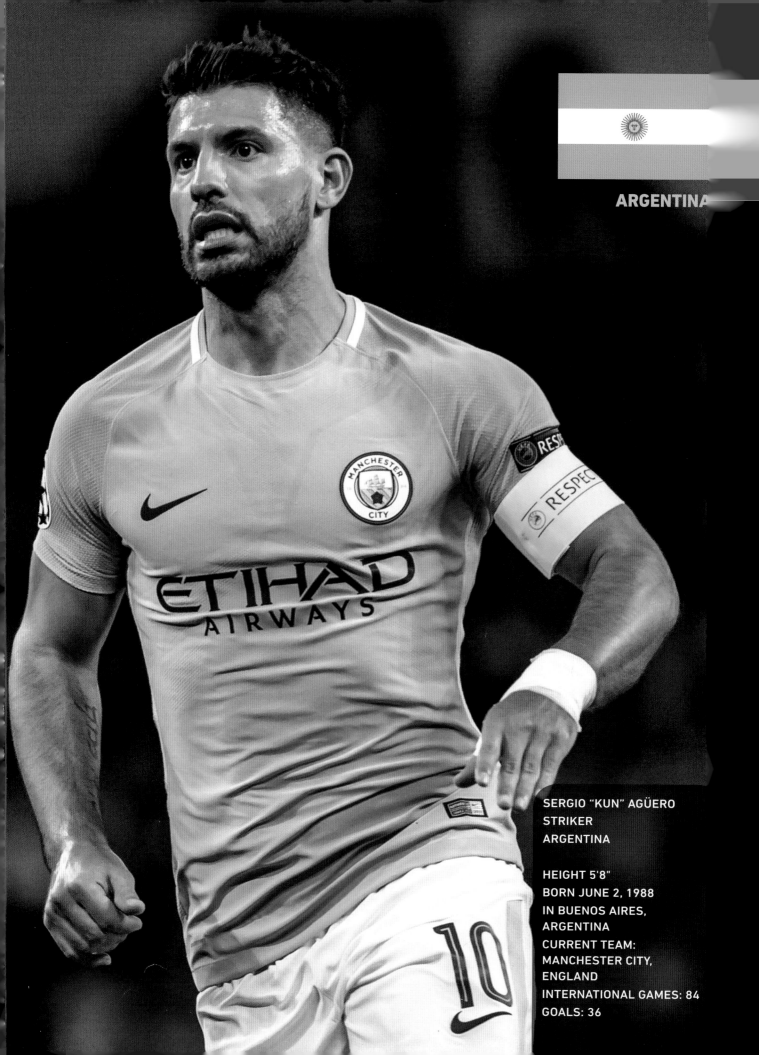

ARGENTINA

SERGIO "KUN" AGÜERO
STRIKER
ARGENTINA

HEIGHT 5'8"
BORN JUNE 2, 1988
IN BUENOS AIRES,
ARGENTINA
CURRENT TEAM:
MANCHESTER CITY,
ENGLAND
INTERNATIONAL GAMES: 84
GOALS: 36

Gareth Bale is left-footed. As a boy, when he was playing soccer with his schoolmates in Cardiff, Wales, the gym teacher would only allow the young Bale to touch the ball with his right foot. The reason for this was that Bale was so much better than all the other boys that his team would always win if he could use his preferred left foot!

This story proves that Bale has always been a great athlete. He was the best in his school in just about every sport and probably could have excelled in all of them.

It's interesting that even though he was so much better then everybody else, there were never any signs of bragging or selfishness in Bale's character or the way he played. His gym teacher said about him: "Gareth is very determined to be successful and has got both the character and the ability to reach his goals. But he's also one of the most unselfish people I have ever worked with."

Fortunately, young Bale finally chose to focus all his energy on soccer, rather than something else. His great pace and technique soon got him noticed, and he became a success as a dynamic left back at Southampton and then later at Tottenham. He's a good shot and has scored many goals in England from free kicks. In 2013, Bale became the world's most expensive soccer player when Real Madrid bought him for $123 million. Even though he's regularly had great spells in Spain, Bale will probably be looking to get back to England in the near future.

BALE

Bale has said that when his career is over, he probably won't have anything to do with soccer: "I don't see myself as the coaching type. I assume I'll be playing a lot of golf when my career is over. I love playing golf."

WALES

GARETH BALE
MIDFIELDER
WALES

HEIGHT 6'1"
BORN JULY 16, 1989
IN CARDIFF, WALES
CURRENT TEAM: REAL
MADRID, SPAIN
INTERNATIONAL GAMES: 70
GOALS: 29

URUGUAY

EDINSON CAVANI
STRIKER
URUGUAY

HEIGHT 6'½"
BORN FEBRUARY 14,1987
IN SALTO, URUGUAY
CURRENT TEAM: PARIS
SAINT-GERMAIN, FRANCE
INTERNATIONAL GAMES: 100
GOALS: 42

In January 2007, a youth version of Copa América was held in Bolivia, for the U-20 national teams of South America. Usually these tournaments don't get a lot of attention, but a few big European clubs sent their scouts anyway. And in the second round a 19-year-old from Uruguay got their attention by scoring a 49th-minute goal against Ecuador. It was a nice goal, but what happened next was more interesting: this 19-year-old just couldn't stop scoring. His team was third in the tournament, but he was the top scorer, with seven goals—one more than a dynamic young player from Chile, Arturo Vidal. The scouts from the big clubs reached for their phones immediately and started telling people about the Uruguayan and his great achievements. During this last decade it has become obvious that what they said about him then was true—he just can't stop scoring.

His name is Edinson Cavani. He comes from a humble background in the city of Salto—just like his compatriot, Luis Suárez, who's the same age—and learned to play soccer in the streets, where things could get quite rough. Cavani learned how to stand on his own two feet, and he adored Gabriel Batistuta, the Argentinian goal machine. When he grew up, Cavani turned out to be quite a similar player to Batistuta—a hard worker, always sniffing out chances in the opponent's box, strong, direct, versatile, able to shoot with both feet, and a great header of the ball. When the big clubs examined him after the tournament, some found him still a bit raw, and he ended up joining Palermo in Italy. In 2010, after a good spell at Palermo, he was snatched up by Napoli, and he also became a regular for his country on the team that ended up fourth in 2010 World Cup in South Africa.

After three years at Napoli (where he scored an amazing 104 goals in 138 games), Cavani went to Paris Saint-Germain.

CAVANI

Cavani is a focused and determined goal scorer. Some thought he might have problems adapting to the other prominent forwards on the PSG team, first Zlatan Ibrahimović and then Neymar. But it really doesn't matter who's playing alongside him, because the end result is always the same—he just can't stop scoring.

For a number of years it has been Liverpool's fate to lose its best players to the big clubs in Spain, even though the fans really want them to stay. The Basque Xabi Alonso went to Real Madrid in 2009, the Argentinian Javier Mascherano went to Barcelona in 2010, and the Uruguayan Luis Suárez went to Barça in 2014. And in the beginning of 2018, the Catalan giants captured yet another genius from the Liverpool team: Philippe Coutinho, the attacking midfielder from Brazil.

Coutinho was born in the metropolis of Rio de Janeiro and grew up only a mile away from the famous Maracaña soccer stadium. Within that stadium, Brazil's highs and lows have played out throughout the years. The young Coutinho learned to play soccer on small futsal courts, where his tiny stature wasn't an issue, because technique and skills were more important. At a young age he caught the attention of the big clubs, and Inter Milan, the Italian giants, signed him when he was only a teenager. In 2010 he played his first game for the Brazilian national team. At Inter, Coutinho didn't fully flourish. His talent was evident, though, and Liverpool signed him in January 2013. Finally, at Liverpool, the young Brazilian managed to live up to his potential and grew into one of the best players in the world.

Coutinho can play as a winger and a striker, but his best position is as a "number 10," a playmaker. His technical abilities are second to none. He's also a good shot, and scored more and more with Liverpool each season. He was happy at Liverpool, but when Barça came calling and wanted him to replace the genius Andrés Iniesta, Coutinho couldn't say no.

COUTINHO

At first, Coutinho found it difficult to nail down a spot on the Brazilian national team, as his role on the team was similar to Neymar's, who was everybody's favorite. Coutinho wasn't on the Brazilian squad for the 2014 World Cup, but there was no question that he'd make the team for the 2018 World Cup in Russia.

PHILIPPE COUTINHO
ATTACKING MIDFIELDER/
WINGER
BRAZIL

HEIGHT 5'7"
BORN JUNE 12, 1992
IN RIO DE JANEIRO, BRAZIL
CURRENT TEAM:
BARCELONA, SPAIN
INTERNATIONAL GAMES: 35
GOALS: 9

BRAZIL

BELGIUM

KEVIN DE BRUYNE
MIDFIELDER
BELGIUM

HEIGHT 5'11"
BORN JUNE 28, 1991
IN DRONGEN, GHENT,
BELGIUM
CURRENT TEAM:
MANCHESTER CITY,
ENGLAND
INTERNATIONAL GAMES: 59
GOALS: 14

Nowadays, two of the world's most famous managers are the Portuguese José Mourinho and the Spaniard Pep Guardiola. In Spain, they were up against each other for long spells, but now both of them are in Manchester, England, where they manage the city's two big Premier League clubs. For most soccer fans, they represent two totally different styles of play. Mourinho's teams are usually highly organized on defense and, when under pressure, happily "park the bus" in front of the goal. Guardiola, on the other hand, represents the sparkling, offensive, tiki-taka style of play, where the team patiently keeps the ball until an opening presents itself.

The treatment of Kevin De Bruyne is an example of the two managers' different approaches. At 21, in his home country of Belgium, De Bruyne's skills had attracted plenty of attention, and he was signed by Chelsea. When Mourinho became the manager of the southwest London team, he didn't know how to utilize the ability of the young player. As a consequence, De Bruyne moved to Germany, where he got his career back on track. Then Manchester City came calling, and since Guardiola arrived at the club, De Bruyne has flourished and is now without doubt one of the world's greatest soccer players.

DE BRUYNE

De Bruyne has many excellent qualities. He's physically strong, a fighter who marks his territory on the field. But he also has great vision and reads the game incredibly well. He's always in search of forward play, and some of his passes to his teammates are downright sublime. In addition, De Bruyne is a great goal scorer, and his goals are often of the most spectacular kind. He scores about one goal every three games.

SPAIN

DAVID DE GEA
GOALKEEPER
SPAIN

HEIGHT 6'4"
BORN NOVEMBER 7, 1990
IN MADRID, SPAIN
CURRENT TEAM:
MANCHESTER UNITED,
ENGLAND
INTERNATIONAL GAMES: 27

Ever since Sir Alex Ferguson retired from the managerial post at Manchester United in spring 2013, things have been rather unstable at this famous club. Manchester United hasn't won the Premier League since and sometimes hasn't even qualified for the Champions League. Also, it's been said that the team doesn't play as aggressively or courageously as it did under Sir Alex.

But even though the team's performance has been somewhat fluctuating, one man has always done his job. In fact, he's saved more points than anyone else on the team. This player is De Gea, the Spanish goalkeeper. Countless times, his spectacular saves have stopped his team from losing or drawing, and without him, United probably would have sunk even deeper during the difficult first years after Sir Alex left. He is the core of the team that José Mourinho started building in 2016.

De Gea showed potential at a very young age. He was born in Madrid, joined Atlético at 13, and was still just a teenager when the English teams QPR and Wigan tried to sign him. But at only 18 he played his first match for Atlético and soon became the team's number one keeper. Sir Alex Ferguson was fascinated by De Gea and put a lot of effort into getting him to United in 2011. In a way, the Spanish goalkeeper was the manager's farewell gift to the club he had made so incredibly successful.

DE GEA

De Gea is a reserved person, and sometimes it seems like he doesn't want to intrude. But he's always ready on the field, with very strong feet and nerves of steel—nothing seems to put him off balance. "This kid is ice cold. He's like a wolf. He's got composure, mental strength, and self-confidence. The pressure some others might feel doesn't affect him at all," said the Atlético goalkeeper coach about his protégé, when De Gea was just 20 years old.

OUSMANE DEMBÉLÉ
FORWARD
FRANCE

HEIGHT 5'10"
BORN MAY 15, 1997
IN VERNON, FRANCE
CURRENT TEAM:
BARCELONA, SPAIN
INTERNATIONAL GAMES: 9
GOALS: 1

DEMBÉLÉ

It came as a great surprise when Neymar, the Brazilian superstar, decided to go from Barcelona to Paris Saint-Germain for a record fee in the summer of 2017. Even more surprising was Barcelona's replacement for Neymar, brought in to play alongside Messi and Suárez, and the money the team offered for that replacement. As it turns out, Barcelona paid $130 million for a relatively inexperienced Frenchman, known only to those who had closely followed French and German soccer. At this point, he had played one season at Dortmund after his switch from the French side Rennes.

This young man's name is Ousmane Dembélé, and the beginning of his Barcelona career was not very good. He got injured in his first league match and was sidelined for four months. As soon as he returned to the field, he got injured again and was out for a few weeks. Hence,

the Camp Nou's demanding crowd had to wait a while before seeing what all that money was spent on. Unlike teams in England, which are owned by various multimillionaires, teams like Barcelona and Real Madrid are owned by the fans, who therefore have a right to be demanding!

However, those who had followed young Dembélé's career and had seen him play for Rennes and Dortmund clearly understood what Barcelona's representatives saw in him. Dembélé is quite similiar to the even younger Kylian Mbappé, who plays for PSG; both came through the fantastic youth system set up by the French soccer association. In special academies located around the country, young and promising players get the opportunity to develop. There, Dembélé could work on his main attributes: pace, technique, and offensive play. He's more like Ronaldo than Messi, as he likes to run at defenses with pace rather then dribble his way through, but he'll probably soon learn the latter from Messi!

Dembélé's origins can be traced to the old French colonies in Africa, as is the case with many French soccer players. His mother is of Senegalese and Mauritanian descent, and his father comes from Mali.

Sometimes soccer is strange. Some people say that Messi can't possibly be called the best soccer player in history, because he's never won the World Cup. But it's quite possible that Messi and his Argentinian teammates would have won the 2014 World Cup in Brazil, if Ángel Di María hadn't been injured in a game against Belgium.

Winger Ángel Di María was born in the city of Rosario, roughly six months after Messi. They never knew each other growing up, but both rose from humble beginnings. Di María's prodigious soccer skills got him out of poverty, and at 19 he signed for Benfica in Portugal, where he was soon noticed for his great crosses from the right wing, along with his overall ability and artistry. In 2010 he signed with Real Madrid, where he lived up to his name and played like an "angel" on the right wing for four years.

Then came the World Cup in Brazil. Although leading up to the tournament Di María had been injured, he played very well in the group stages and sent Argentina into the quarterfinals by scoring the only goal against Switzerland. In the next game, he made the assist to Gonzalo Higuaín, who scored the winning goal, but then Di María got injured and had to come off. The Argentinian team was badly hit by the loss of their creative winger for the rest of the tournament, and in the final against Germany it became obvious how much Messi missed Di María. Messi just couldn't score, and Germany won.

Next, Di María made a big-money move to Manchester United, but for a number of reasons, it didn't turn out well. Manager Louis van Gaal didn't seem to know how to use this elegant player. In 2015, Di María moved to Paris Saint-Germain, where he has established himself as one of the most exciting wingers in world soccer.

DI MARÍA

In the summer of 2017, Di María came close to joining Barcelona, where he could have played alongside his compatriot and friend Lionel Messi. In Di María's words: "There are no words to describe Messi; he constantly catches you by surprise. Cristiano Ronaldo is a great player, but Messi is from another planet."

ARGENTINA

ÁNGEL DI MARÍA
ATTACKING MIDFIELDER/
WINGER
ARGENTINA

HEIGHT 5'10"
BORN FEBRUARY 14, 1988
IN ROSARIO, ARGENTINA
CURRENT TEAM: PARIS
SAINT-GERMAIN, FRANCE
INTERNATIONAL GAMES: 92
GOALS: 19

On his game, Eden Hazard can be just as good as Lionel Messi. This clever Belgian is short, with a low center of gravity, which allows him to be very balanced and strong at the same time. He can penetrate the most powerful defenses with such artistry that it reminds people of the famous Argentinian. Hazard also has a great eye for passes and spaces, and he's a good shot. The only thing that prevents him from being Messi's equal, instead of "merely" one of the 5 or 10 best soccer players in the world, is that he can sometimes make mistakes and have an off day. Hazard's performances were great when Chelsea won the Premier League title in the spring of 2015, but he wasn't able to change his team's fortunes during the next season. When Hazard is on form, though, he's almost unbeatable. This he proved when Chelsea once again won the Premier League title in

the 2016–2017 season. He scored 17 goals and made many assists. The next season things were not as stable at the club, but Hazard always did his best.

For the past few years, the Belgian national team has been one of the best in the world. Hazard's magnificent ability is an important asset, but many other great players come from this small country, including De Bruyne, Lukaku, Vertonghen, and the goalkeeper Courtois. Even with all this talent, the Belgian national team disappointed in the 2014 World Cup and the 2016 Euro finals. After the Euro finals, the Belgians have put all their focus on the 2018 World Cup, which they desperately want to win. With players like De Bruyne on the team, anything is possible, but one of the most important things will be getting Hazard firing on all cylinders. Then, the sky's the limit.

HAZARD

Compared to most others, Hazard got to know soccer quite early, as his mother played as a striker on a Belgian team during the first months of her pregnancy. His father was also a soccer player, and his younger brother, Thorgan, has played a few games with the Belgian national team. Hazard lives and breathes soccer, and has bought an American soccer team, San Diego 1904, with fellow players including Demba Ba and Yohan Cabaye.

BELGIUM

EDEN HAZARD
FORWARD/WINGER
BELGIUM

HEIGHT 5'8"
BORN JANUARY 7, 1991
IN LA LOUVIÈRE, BELGIUM
CURRENT TEAM: CHELSEA,
ENGLAND
INTERNATIONAL GAMES: 82
GOALS: 21

ANDRÉS INIESTA
MIDFIELDER
SPAIN

HEIGHT 5'7½"
BORN MAY 11, 1984
IN FUENTEALBILLA, SPAIN
CURRENT TEAM:
BARCELONA, SPAIN
INTERNATIONAL GAMES: 124
GOALS: 13

INIESTA

Andrés Iniesta was was born in a small village of two thousand people in the mountainous province of Albacete in the center of Spain. Playing at a boys' soccer tournament in Albacete at the age of 12, he showed such great skills that scouts from the big clubs became interested. A friend of his parents was a coach at Barcelona's famous academy, La Masia, and got his parents to take him there. Although already a magician with the ball, Iniesta was reserved, shy, and not that keen on moving to the big city, far away from friends and family. He admits to crying his eyes out when saying good-bye to his parents.

Soon, though, the joy of playing soccer got his mind off how much he missed things back home. In that period, Barcelona was developing a specific style of play called tiki-taka, which mainly consisted of a well-rehearsed, fast-paced game of passing and constant pressure when the opponent had the ball. Well-played tiki-taka soccer can be incredibly beautiful to watch, and Iniesta became an excellent representative of that style. He and his friend Xavi controlled both Barcelona's and Spain's midfield, and were the catalysts in Spain's 2008–2012 success, when the national team was the first ever to win three major tournaments in a row.

Xavi has since retired and tiki-taka has evolved, but Iniesta is still playing and threading passes through to Messi, Suárez, and the other Barcelona forwards. And even though he's slowing down a bit, he's still an influential player on the national team and can probably still lead them to new victories.

Maybe Iniesta is too reserved to be a major goal scorer—he'd rather get the ball to other players than penetrate defenses himself. But he has been known to score some spectacular goals, and in fact he scored the most fateful goal in the history of Spanish soccer. This was in the 2010 World Cup final in South Africa, when the free-flowing Spaniards met the defiant Dutch. Iniesta broke the deadlock in extra time, scoring the only goal of the game, and Spain won the World Cup.

Giant Real Madrid is often criticized for buying established superstars from other teams—players who have already proved themselves as the world's best—instead of growing their own Spanish talent. This business model is known as the "galáctico" policy. To many Spaniards, Isco is a welcome exception to this, although he's not originally from Madrid. He was born in Andalusia in the south of Spain and played for Valencia as a youth, but signed for Málaga at 21. Real Madrid snapped him up in 2013, and he's since developed into one of the best players on both the Real Madrid and Spanish teams.

By nature, Isco is a forward-thinking midfielder who knows how to score goals. He's quick and technical, can easily go past players if he needs to, and always seems to anticipate what is about to happen. Presently, as younger players are taking over in the Spanish national team and the heroes from the 2008–2012 era are fading away, Isco is becoming increasingly important, both in conducting offensive play and being a threat himself. He has played as a holding midfielder, as a winger, and even as a striker.

ISCO

Another young Spanish player at Real will probably become one of the team's best, if he continues his current development. This is Marco Asensio, an offensive-minded midfielder and a winger from Mallorca, born in 1996. He's already made his mark on the Real team, and it will be interesting to see his partnership with Isco both there and on the Spanish national side.

SPAIN

ISCO
(FULL NAME FRANCISCO
ROMÁN ALARCÓN SUÁREZ)
ATTACKING MIDFIELDER
SPAIN

HEIGHT 5'10"
BORN APRIL 21, 1992,
IN BENALMÁDENA, SPAIN
CURRENT TEAM: REAL
MADRID, SPAIN
INTERNATIONAL GAMES: 26
GOALS: 10

The 2014 World Cup in Brazil was a great disappointment to the home nation. They had counted on winning their sixth tournament, but after their captain, Neymar, was sidelined because of injuries, the team's performance suffered—they were slow, pedestrian, and lacking a goal scorer. That was something new for the Brazilians, who've had some of the world's most famous goal scorers within their ranks: Leônidas, Adhemar, Pelé, Romário, Ronaldo, and Ronaldinho. All of a sudden, the future wasn't so bright for Brazil.

But now things have changed. Tite, the new coach, has been very successful and has the team playing more entertaining soccer than many of his predecessors. It's starting to resemble the famous "samba soccer," which dates back to the time when players such as Pelé and Zico were on the team. The Brazilians love that kind of play. Neymar keeps getting better, but now a promising young goal scorer has also stepped forward, and the nation expects much of him. His name is Gabriel Jesus.

Jesus was born in the metropolis of São Paulo and played soccer out on the streets when he was a boy. Then he trained with the youth team in his neighborhood. There, he was discovered by scouts from a big club, Palmeiras, and broke onto the first team at only 18 years old. He was considered exceptionally mature for a forward, and very strong and versatile. Consequently, he was soon snatched up by Manchester City, where he's frightened the living daylights out of goalkeepers ever since.

JESUS

In northern European countries, it's considered inappropriate to name people after Jesus Christ, but that's not the case in Spanish- and Portuguese-speaking ones, where Jesus is a common name. (In Brazil, people speak Portuguese.) As it happens, Jesus comes from a religious family and strongly believes in Jesus Christ himself.

BRAZIL

GABRIEL JESUS
STRIKER
SPAIN

HEIGHT 5'9"
BORN APRIL 3, 1997
IN SÃO PAULO, BRAZIL
CURRENT TEAM:
MANCHESTER CITY,
ENGLAND
INTERNATIONAL GAMES: 15
GOALS: 9

It's been a while since an English player has been considered among the best in the world. Players such as Wayne Rooney, Steven Gerrard, David Beckham, and Paul Scholes might have been, but they peaked 10 to 20 years ago—and not everyone would agree that they were truly among the best of the best.

To find a player in the English shirt who was indisputably world class, you'd probably have to go all the way back to Gary Lineker—up until now, that is.

Harry Kane is fast becoming one of the most dangerous strikers in world soccer, playing for Tottenham Hotspur and the English national team.

Kane's career is interesting.

During his first years at Spurs, Kane went on loan to lower-league teams. He wasn't that successful there, either. But then in the spring of 2014 Kane scored in three successive games, and during the 2014–2015 season it was like he was on fire. Under new Spurs manager Mauricio Pochettino, Kane just couldn't stop scoring. He was the Premier League's second-highest scorer, with 21 goals in 34 games, as well as in all competitions, with 31 goals in 51 games.

Over the past few years, Kane has shown that this was no accident. The goals he scores can come from inside or outside the box, and they can come from headers. He can use both feet, dribble past players, or make calculated runs in behind the defense. He's the complete striker.

As a person, he's quiet and well

He was never a wunderkind, and Arsenal released him from academy when he was nine. He managed to get a contract at Tottenham, but the club didn't seem to have much faith in him at first. He came across as somewhat clumsy and wasn't particularly fast or physically strong. And nobody knew what his best position was yet.

mannered. He doesn't say much, buts lets his playing speak for itself. Although Tottenham is a great club, it wasn't long before people started wondering if Kane should be playing for a bigger club on an even larger stage.

KANE

ENGLAND

After the 2016 Euro finals in France, Kane felt tired—so tired, in fact, that he came to the conclusion something was not right. As it turned out, the defeat against Iceland wasn't the reason, but rather an unhealthy diet. Kane hired a special chef to prepare, cook, and serve his meals in order to maximize his health and performance.

Toni Kroos is not a flamboyant soccer player. He's a midfielder who likes to get the ball from defenders and pass it on to more forward-thinking midfielders and strikers. In this role he's a true genius; not many players can execute such great ball distribution. He can of course also go forward and score himself, and Kroos's goals are often quite spectacular efforts from long range, coming out of nowhere and placed with great precision. His long-range passes invariably end up exactly where they're supposed to, and that's why "precise" is usually the first word people use to describe Toni Kroos.

Kroos was born in a medium-sized town in the eastern part of Germany, but scouts from Bayern Munich noticed him and brought him west. In 2007, when he had just turned 17, Kroos became the youngest man to ever play for Bayern. Coming in as a sub in his first game, he instantly showed what could be expected of him by creating two goals for his teammates. He then became a part of Bayern's victorious group of midfielders and won many titles. Soon, he also grew into a vital part of the tremendously strong German national team, which won the 2014 World Cup in Brazil. When Germany thrashed Brazil 7–1 in one of the most incredible games ever played in a World Cup tournament, Man of the Match Kroos came up with two goals and one assist.

He then went to Spain, where he has controlled Real Madrid's midfield alongside Luka Modrić, and nobody on the Madrid team wants to lose him.

KROOS

Kroos's talent is such that he can play all the midfield positions, as well as building up offensive play. He can operate as a defensive midfielder or a winger, break up the opposition's play, keep the ball, and create opportunities for others. In 2014, the Dutch soccer genius Johan Cruyff said this about Kroos's performance in the World Cup: "He's doing everything right. The pace in his passing is great, and he sees everything. It's nearly perfect."

TONI KROOS
MIDFIELDER
GERMANY

HEIGHT 6'
BORN JANUARY 4, 1990 IN
GREIFSWALD, GERMANY
CURRENT TEAM: REAL
MADRID, SPAIN
INTERNATIONAL GAMES: 82
GOALS: 12

LEWANDOWSKI

On September 22, 2015, one of the most unbelievable things in soccer history happened. Bayern Munich was playing Wolfsburg in the Allianz Arena, and was trailing 0–1 at halftime. Bayern's manager Pep Guardiola was not happy and made a substitution. On came the big, strong Polish striker Robert Lewandowski, playing in his second season for Bayern after coming over from Dortmund, where he'd scored about 30 goals a season for the past few years. Obviously, nobody doubted his ability to score goals, but what happened in that second half was almost ridiculous.

In the 51st minute, he received the ball in front of Wolfsburg's goal and easily put it in the back of the net, thereby tying the game. It was his first touch of the game. A minute later the Pole scored his second goal, with an unexpected shot from outside the box. It came from nowhere. In the 55th minute Lewandowski hit the post, but then somehow managed to scramble the ball over the line, scoring the quickest hat trick in Bundesliga history.

In the 57th minute the ball entered the box from the left, and Lewandowski arrived swiftly, hit a superb volley, and hammered the ball into the back of the net. And it wasn't over yet, because in the 60th minute, Lewandowski was on the receiving end of a Mario Götze pass at the edge of the penalty area and sliced the ball beautifully into the net—his fifth and best goal. Nobody has ever scored five goals in nine minutes, let alone as a substitute. This goes to show that Lewandowski is an incredible goal scorer and can do almost anything.

Lewandowski was born into an athletic family: His father competed in judo and played soccer, and his mother and sister played volleyball. Lewandowski's wife also competes in karate!

POLAND

ROBERT LEWANDOWSKI
STRIKER
POLAND

HEIGHT 6'1"
BORN AUGUST 21, 1988
IN WARSAW, POLAND
CURRENT TEAM: BAYERN
MUNICH, GERMANY
INTERNATIONAL GAMES: 93
GOALS: 52

FRANCE

KYLIAN MBAPPÉ
FORWARD
FRANCE

HEIGHT 5'10"
BORN DECEMBER 20, 1988
IN PARIS, FRANCE
CURRENT TEAM: PARIS
SAINT-GERMAIN, FRANCE
INTERNATIONAL GAMES: 12
GOALS: 3

Kylian Mbappé played his first game for the French team Monaco in 2015, at the age of only 16, and immediately became known for his technical ability. It was not until 2017, however, that he established himself on the world stage as one of soccer's most exciting talents. That year, when he became a regular on the Monaco team, they won the French league title, and Mbappé scored 26 goals in 44 games.

French soccer enthusiasts had heard of Mbappé long before this all took place, however. He was still just a boy when people inside the French academies were heaping praise on him. His offensive and technical ability earned him comparisons to one of France's most prolific goal scorers of all time, Thierry Henry. And because Mbappé is more mature than Henry was at the same age, he could become even better!

Many big clubs were keeping an eye on Mbappé, but he decided to go to Monaco, which he considered the ideal place to start his career. And the 2016–2017 season was unbelievable. The fact that a 17-to 18-year-old scored 26 goals in 44 games strongly indicated the birth of a new genius.

Monaco knew they wouldn't be able to keep him, so they loaned him to Paris Saint-Germain instead of selling him. There, he has played alongside Neymar and scored goals like there's no tomorrow. In the future, it's going to be a lot of fun watching Mbappé and Ousmane Dembélé playing together for the French national team.

MBAPPÉ

Mbappé's father is a soccer coach from Cameroon. His mother comes from Algeria and played handball when she was young. When Mbappé was growing up, Cristiano Ronaldo was his idol, and their main attributes are quite similar—like the Portuguese, the young Frenchman is lightning quick, a good shot, and very offensive.

LIONEL MESSI
FORWARD
ARGENTINA

HEIGHT 5'7"
BORN JUNE 24, 1987
IN ROSARIO, SANTA FE,
ARGENTINA
CURRENT TEAM: BARCELONA,
SPAIN
INTERNATIONAL GAMES: 146
GOALS: 77

Leo Messi is probably the best soccer player ever to have walked the earth. He has set so many goal-scoring records and won so many prizes that only one other player can be regarded as a rival in that respect: Cristiano Ronaldo. But the way he has achieved this is just as important—Messi is a true soccer artist. He brings joy and happiness to fans not only when scoring spectacular goals, but also in open play, with what can only be described as magic tricks. It's not throwing shade over great athletes such as Cristiano Ronaldo or the Brazilian Ronaldo to say that Messi's artistic wizardry is better then anything they've ever offered. Perhaps it's possible, at some level, to compare Messi to the Brazilian Ronaldinho, who used to delight the fans with his constant trickery. But when it comes to goal scoring and overall consistency, Messi towers over Ronaldinho. Messi is now 30 and therefore entering the latter stages of his career. But for now, he shows no signs of decline, and soccer fans should simply enjoy his genius while it's still on show.

ARGENTINA

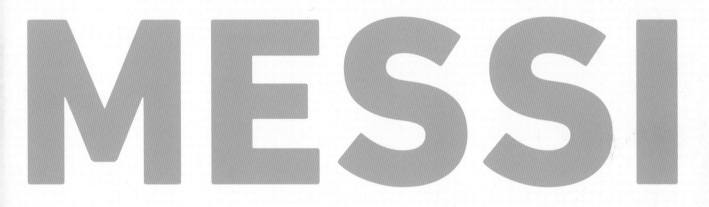

MESSI

Like his archrival Cristiano Ronaldo and many other soccer players, Messi was found guilty of tax fraud. With such astronomically high salaries, in addition to their other income such as sponsorship deals, it's difficult to understand why wealthy soccer players feel the need to avoid paying taxes. Messi himself wasn't directly involved in fraud, as his father handles his finances, but he is considered legally responsible for the payment of his taxes and received a suspended sentence for this first offense.

Croatia is one of Europe's smaller and more sparsely populated countries. It's around 21,851 square miles, and has a population of roughly four million. The country is known for its great sporting traditions, especially when it comes to ball sports. For most of the twentieth century Croatia was a part of Yugoslavia, which came in third in the 1930 World Cup, and second in the Euro finals in 1960 and 1968. The Croatian national team has been doing quite well since the country became independent. They usually qualify for the big tournaments, and often play with gusto. Croatia came in third in the 1998 World Cup in France.

The fact that Croatians Luka Modrić and Ivan Rakitić are key midfield players for Real Madrid and Barcelona, respectively, says everything about how good Croatian soccer players really are. Modrić has been influential in Real's success over the past few years, even if he's not as prominent as forwards such as Cristiano Ronaldo, Gareth Bale, and Karim Benzema. But many of their goals come after accurate assists from Modrić. That's what he does best—building up play from the middle of the field and delivering balls to the forwards. Few players are as focused and skillful as Modrić when it comes to this.

The only criticism you can possibly make about Modrić is that he's not selfish enough. Without a doubt, he could score many more goals himself—he definitely has the ability and power to do so—but he just seems to enjoy passing the ball to others more.

MODRIĆ

Modrić gained attention in Croatia for his skills, but no one really knew if he'd amount to anything, because he was so small and slight. (In Croatia it's usually the bigger players who get ahead.) But Modrić kept playing to his strengths, and Tottenham ended up offering him a contract in 2008. At White Hart Lane, the little Croatian showed what he was capable of and then went to Real in 2012 to become a world star.

LUKA MODRIĆ
MIDFIELDER
CROATIA

HEIGHT 5'8"
BORN SEPTEMBER 9, 1985
IN ZADAR, CROATIA
CURRENT TEAM: REAL
MADRID, SPAIN
INTERNATIONAL GAMES: 104
GOALS: 12

GERMANY

MANUEL NEUER
GOALKEEPER
GERMANY

HEIGHT 6'4"
BORN MARCH 27, 1986
IN GELSENKIRCHEN,
GERMANY
CURRENT TEAM: BAYERN
MUNICH, GERMANY
INTERNATIONAL GAMES: 74

Neuer was a promising athlete as a boy. He was a great tennis player, although soccer came out on top in the end. On youth teams, before he decided to focus on the goalkeeping position, Neuer regularly played in outfield positions. Neuer's brother was also a soccer player, but retired early and is now a lower-league referee.

The German national team is known for great goalkeepers: the magnificent Sepp Maier, the controversial Harald Schumacher, and the rivals Jens Lehmann and Oliver Kahn. It says a lot about Manuel Neuer's strength and talent that many think he's the best keeper of them all. Some even say Neuer is simply the best goalkeeper the world has ever seen.

Neuer is known for his courageous runs outside the box and for taking the ball far up the field before he passes it on to one of his teammates. He's got an imposing build and incredibly strong hands and feet, but is also surprisingly slick and clever. He started his career playing for Schalke in Gelsenkirchen, his hometown, but joined the big boys in Bayern Munich in 2011. And because Bayern are such a dominant team, Neuer sometimes has long spells of waiting and watching the game. But he's always alert and intervenes when needed, pouncing like a cat.

Neuer is one of the main reasons Germany won its fifth World Cup in 2014, beating Argentina 1–0 in the final. Neuer closed the goal, and Messi and his teammates couldn't find a way through. He was voted the best goalkeeper of the tournament, and the third-best player in the world at the Ballon d'Or ceremony, after Cristiano Ronaldo and Messi. It's rare to see a goalkeeper so high on the list. Ever since the World Cup in Brazil, it's been Neuer's dream to lead his team to another World Cup victory.

NEUER

BRAZIL

NEYMAR
(FULL NAME NEYMAR
DA SILVA SANTOS JÚNIOR)
FORWARD
BRAZIL

HEIGHT 5'9"
BORN FEBRUARY 5, 1992
IN MOGI DAS CRUZES, SÃO
PAULO, BRAZIL
CURRENT TEAM: PARIS
SAINT-GERMAIN, FRANCE
INTERNATIONAL GAMES: 83
GOALS: 53

In spring 2017, Neymar, the Brazilian wizard, seemed on top of the world. As a member of the famous Barcelona team, he was adored and respected, and his teammates up front were Messi and Suárez. Although the season before hadn't been great, it was considered only a minor dip in the trio's ongoing success.

But then Neymar made an unexpected move. He joined Paris Saint-Germain in France for a record $263 million. For sure, PSG was a rich club and had many fine players, but the French Ligue 1 is by no means as strong as the Spanish La Liga, and PSG had not been that successful in the Champions League. Even Neymar's father, who is also his close friend and advisor, was against the idea of him moving to Paris.

Although Neymar was good friends with Messi and Suárez, his mindset was such that he would never be able to accept not being his team's main man. That's why Neymar went to PSG, although it remains uncertain if he'll stay there for long. Many think he'll end up at Barcelona's archenemy, Real Madrid.

At PSG, the gifted forward had no problem scoring goals and becoming the undoubted star of the team. He's also been influential on the Brazilian national team, which hasn't been this good for many years. The 2014 World Cup in Brazil was a colossal disappointment to both Neymar and the home side as a whole, so now the aim is to win the 2018 World Cup in style. And Neymar, at the age of 26, has the best years of his career ahead of him. Seriously, how far can he go?

NEYMAR

When Neymar left Barça, Messi sent him a message on Twitter: "It's been an absolute pleasure sharing these years with you, my friend. I wish you all the best in this next stage of your life. See you soon." And Neymar responded: "Thanks, brother. I will miss you."

SPAIN

GERARD PIQUÉ
DEFENDER
SPAIN

HEIGHT 6'4"
BORN FEBRUARY 2, 1987
IN BARCELONA, SPAIN
CURRENT TEAM:
BARCELONA, SPAIN
INTERNATIONAL GAMES: 96
GOALS: 5

Gerard Piqué brings joy to the fans wherever he plays. He's a tall and prominent defender, has a good positional sense, is a great tackler, and reads the game well. But the most fun part of his game is when he goes strolling forward, which is something he's allowed to do, as he often creates danger with his runs. He usually scores between three and seven goals a season, which is good for a center back, and he's also a big part of the famous and entertaining Barcelona style of play.

Piqué is now a force on the Barcelona defense similar to the great Carles Puyol of some 10 to 15 years ago. Piqué almost ended up playing abroad, though. He was in Leo Messi and Cesc Fàbregas's class in La Masia, the Barcelona academy, but was lured into moving to Manchester United when he was just 17. Alex Ferguson was never convinced about him, though, and while Piqué played a number of games for United in the 2007–2008 season, he never felt like he had a future at Old Trafford. He went back to Barcelona and immediately became a regular in the starting 11, at only 21 years of age. He was also chosen to play for his country, and it was a proud moment for the young Barcelona native to be alongside Puyol in the heart of the Spanish defense against Holland in the 2010 World Cup.

Despite Piqué's marvelous achievements in the red shirt of Spain, he has been frustrating some of the fans lately. The reason for that is simple—Barcelona is in Catalonia, and Piqué supports the cause of Catalan independence, which is a contested issue in Spain.

PIQUÉ

Piqué is the first soccer player—maybe since David Beckham and his wife Victoria were on the scene—who has a spouse who's both richer and more famous than he is. Piqué's wife, the Colombian singer Shakira, has sold more than 100 million albums all over the world and is especially popular in Spanish-speaking countries. They met when Piqué appeared in the video for her 2010 World Cup song, "Waka Waka (This Time for Africa)," and they have two sons.

PAUL POGBA
MIDFIELDER
FRANCE

HEIGHT 6'2"
BORN MARCH 15, 1993
IN LAGNY-SUR-MARNE,
FRANCE
CURRENT TEAM:
MANCHESTER UNITED,
ENGLAND
INTERNATIONAL GAMES: 51
GOALS: 9

Pogba has older twin brothers, born in 1990. Both of them are fine soccer players, even though they're not quite as good as their younger brother Paul. Both have played for the national team of Guinea, the West African country where their parents are from.

POGBA

Paul Pogba, along with Gerard Piqué, the Barcelona defender, is one of the very few players Sir Alex Ferguson didn't rate correctly. In 2009, in his home country of France, Pogba played for the Le Havre and French national youth teams. He was already a tall, powerful, offensive, and versatile midfielder. Then, Manchester United offered him a spot within its academy, which Pogba accepted, much to the annoyance of Le Havre's executives, who thought they already had a deal with him. But when push came to shove, Pogba didn't feel appreciated at Manchester United. Ferguson rarely used him, and as a consequence, in 2012, Pogba would not sign a new deal and headed over to Juventus instead. And for the next few years, in a Juve shirt, he would show just what he was capable of.

Pogba proved himself and soon became the talisman of Juventus, who were incredibly strong at the time—the team won the Italian league title during all four seasons that Pogba spent there, the Italian Cup twice, and was runner-up in the Champions League in 2015. Now the Manchester United executives realized they had made a big mistake by letting Pogba leave, and in August 2016 they bought him back. The fee was enormous—around $130 million. At the time, Pogba was the most expensive player in the world, although that's not the case anymore. United's manager, José Mourinho, admires spirited players like Pogba and will certainly build his team around the Frenchman in the future. Pogba has also become the dynamo of the French national team. Although he and his French teammates failed to win the European title in front of their home crowd in the summer of 2016—they lost to a highly resilient Portugal side in the final—the future of French soccer is very bright, with young and promising goal scorers coming onto an already excellent team.

SPAIN

HEIGHT 6'
BORN MARCH 30, 1986
IN CAMAS, SPAIN
CURRENT TEAM: REAL
MADRID, SPAIN
INTERNATIONAL GAMES: 151
GOALS: 13

SPAIN

Sergio Ramos is the kind of defender fans love. He's not particularly tall, but is very strong and nimble. His movements are quick, and when he gets going, his pace is incredible—in 2015 he measured as one of the world's fastest soccer players. Ramos is well known for his ability to head the ball—not many players can match him in the air—and he scores lots of goals. Since he joined Real from Sevilla in 2005, he's scored around 70 goals, most of them with headers. The moment he scored his first goal in the 2017–2018 season, on February 3, 2018 (with a header, of course!), he became the first defender to score 14 seasons in a row.

As a player, Ramos is both extremely tough and passionate. He never gives up and often gets into trouble because of his competitive nature. In December 2017, he got the 19th red card of his career, which is a record in Spain. His fouls are rarely that brutal, and he hasn't caused other players serious injuries, but he can lose his temper completely. Despite the risk of him being sent off, Ramos was made Real Madrid's captain, as he consistently spurs his teammates on and the atmosphere is always lively around him.

Obviously, strength and power are not the only attributes that Ramos has at his disposal. He also tackles with great precision, plays out of the back superbly, and can even support the attack and deliver crosses from the wings. But even so, the best thing about Ramos is his great fighting spirit!

RAMOS

Sergio Ramos doesn't have to worry about what to do when his career ends. He's an avid equestrian and owner of a horse ranch in his home region, where he breeds Andalusian thoroughbreds.

RONALDO

There's a lot that can be said about Cristiano Ronaldo, but the main thing is he never lacks motivation or the ability to reach his goals. He was voted the world's best soccer player in 2008 (winning the Ballon d'Or, the "Golden Ball") and won both the Premier League and the Champions League with Manchester United. It seemed like he would to be recognized as the world's greatest player for many years to come.

During the following years he kept on scoring and broke many records, especially after he joined Real Madrid in 2009. But unfortunately for Ronaldo, the Argentinian maestro, Lionel Messi, had suddenly appeared and was voted the world's best soccer player four years in a row! Nobody had done that before, and Ronaldo seemed stuck in second place.

However, Ronaldo is known for his incredible determination, and he didn't give up. He wanted to be recognized as the best and managed to win the Ballon d'Or for the next two years running. Then, Messi was voted the world's best soccer player for the fifth time, and surely no one could follow in his footsteps. But Ronaldo did exactly that by winning the Ballon d'Or twice in a row again, so now the archrivals have won soccer's most prestigious individual prize five times each.

It's hard to say if Ronaldo can win the prize again. He's two years older than Messi, and at some point, the unbelievable energy he puts into his training must inevitably take its toll. As a player, Ronaldo is more limited than Messi. He is a goal scorer first and foremost, and not as creative as the Argentinian. But that doesn't make his achievements any less impressive, and people will remember them for many years to come.

Cristiano Ronaldo was born on the small island of Madeira, where he grew up in poverty, although his family never went hungry. His father was an alcoholic, and family life suffered as a consequence. This young man used soccer to rise above his family difficulties, show his immense ability and value, and reach the very top.

CRISTIANO RONALDO DOS
SANTOS AVEIRO
FORWARD
PORTUGAL

HEIGHT 6'1"
BORN FEBRUARY 5, 1985
IN FUNCHAL, MADEIRA,
PORTUGAL
CURRENT TEAM: REAL
MADRID, SPAIN
INTERNATIONAL GAMES: 149
GOALS: 81

EGYPT

MOHAMED SALAH
FORWARD
EGYPT

HEIGHT 5'9"
BORN JUNE 15, 1992
IN NAGRIG, GHARBIA, EGYPT
CURRENT TEAM: LIVERPOOL,
ENGLAND
INTERNATIONAL GAMES: 57
GOALS: 33

For doing so well in the English Premier League, and more importantly, for getting his country to the World Cup, Salah is a national hero in Egypt. An Egyptian millionaire wanted to give Salah a luxury palace for the goals he scored against Congo, but Salah has not forgotten his humble background. He asked the millionaire to donate the value of the palace to Salah's small, struggling hometown instead. A children's school in Egypt has already been named after Salah, as have many streets.

SALAH

Egyptians are fanatic when it comes to soccer, but as yet they've not enjoyed great international success. They've won the Africa Cup of Nations a few times, but have never put their marker down in a World Cup tournament. Therefore, the whole nation celebrated wildly when the national team got through to the 2018 World Cup in Russia by beating Congo 2–1 in October 2017. And to top things off, both the goals were scored by Liverpool's little genius, Mohamed Salah. The Egyptians trust Salah will lead them to glory in the World Cup—and his skills are so incredible that no one will be surprised if he ends up as the tournament's top scorer. Salah is an offensive-minded player who has almost everything a great forward needs. He's extremely fast, has good positional awareness, and is very clever when it comes to finding spaces from where he can make direct runs in behind the defense. He's a marvelous addition to Jürgen Klopp's offensive Liverpool team and has quickly become every Liverpool supporter's idol. In his first season, he broke all the goal-scoring records previously set by Liverpool's new players.

José Mourinho didn't see Salah's brilliance while he was playing for Chelsea a few years ago. The Portuguese manager could find little use for him and in the end off-loaded him to Italy, where he became a huge success. Even so, when Salah moved to Liverpool, nobody suspected such a force of nature would be unleashed.

SÁNCHEZ

CHILE

ALEXIS SÁNCHEZ
FORWARD/WINGER
CHILE

HEIGHT 5'6"
BORN DECEMBER 19, 1988
IN TOCOPILLA, CHILE
CURRENT TEAM:
MANCHESTER UNITED,
ENGLAND
INTERNATIONAL GAMES: 119
GOALS: 39

Chile has never been one of soccer's elite nations. It was third in the 1962 World Cup, when the tournament was played in Chile, but apart from that the national team did not do well, and often failed to qualify. And for a long time, Chile had never won the Copa América. However, Chile finally developed a very strong team around 2010 and won the 2015 and 2016 Copa América by beating Messi's Argentina in a penalty shoot-out on both occasions. The people of Chile were hoping this generation of players would be successful in the 2018 World Cup, with the likes of goalkeeper Claudio Bravo (Manchester City), midfielder Arturo Vidal (Bayern Munich), and of course, the dynamic forward Alexis Sánchez. Leading up to the 2018 World Cup in Russia, everything was going well, but then Chile surprisingly lost three of their four final games in the group and didn't qualify.

Many were sad to see the Chileans—especially the entertaining Sánchez—left out. He's a truly passionate player: offensive-minded, hardworking, and relentless. In addition, he's got quite a temper. He is all smiles when everything is going his way, but doesn't try to hide his emotions when they are not. However, he never gives up.

Sánchez established himself as a major talent with Udinese in Italy and was, as a consequence, snatched up by Barcelona. There, he scored in roughly every third game, but never integrated fully into the team. He made a switch to Arsenal in 2014. With the English outfit he scored many goals, including 30 in 51 games during the 2016–2017 season. But he thought that moving to the north of England to play for Manchester United would give him a better chance of winning silverware, and forced a move to that club in January 2018.

Sánchez was born in a relatively small town called Tocopilla, in Chile. It has long been a hotbed for Chilean soccer talent, and three established players on the national team, Sánchez included, come from Tocopilla. But Sánchez is clearly the best, as can be seen by the fact that a statue of him has been raised on a scenic spot in town.

There was a time when David Silva stood in the shadows of geniuses such as Xavi, Iniesta, Fernando Torres, and David Villa. He did play a part in the incredible success of the Spanish team that won three major tournaments in a row (Euro 2008, World Cup 2010, Euro 2012), but in the first two tournaments his role was a minor one. In the 2012 Euro finals, however, he had become a regular on the team and scored the first goal in a 4–0 victory against Italy in the final. He was involved in more goals than any other player in the tournament, scoring two and making three assists.

Silva then joined England's Manchester City, where each season he has become better and even more important to the team. He's a natural "number 10"—a player who operates just behind the front man, lures the defenders in with his skills, and then quickly delivers accurate passes behind the line, or scores himself with neat shots, or dribbles through the opponent's defense. He's simply a hard worker, always on the lookout for chances, and playing with grace and power. When Pep Guardiola came to Manchester City, Silva got a manager who truly appreciated him, and knew how to exploit his incredible ability.

Now, with Xavi, Torres, and Villa gone from Spain's lineup and Iniesta slowing down a bit, it's important that Silva manage the team's offensive play, while allowing young and promising players such as Isco and Marco Asensio to get the experience they need.

SILVA

DAVID SILVA
MIDFIELDER
SPAIN

HEIGHT 5'8"
BORN JANUARY 8, 1986
IN ARGUINEGUÍN, SPAIN
CURRENT TEAM:
MANCHESTER CITY,
ENGLAND
INTERNATIONAL GAMES: 118
GOALS: 35

In December 2017, a traumatic event occurred in David Silva's life: his son Mateo was born prematurely, and it was not known if he would survive. Silva took a leave of absence to be with his family, with good wishes from colleagues pouring in. Fortunately, by May 2018 baby Mateo was strong enough to leave the hospital.

In the beginning, Luis Suárez was constant trouble. Nobody doubted his talent in front of the goal, but he just couldn't seem to control himself on the field. At a very young age, he made the switch from Uruguay's Nacional to the Netherlands' Groningen and once scored four goals in five games for them. But in those same five games, he also got three yellow cards and one red! He then went to Ajax, where he kept on collecting cards and was—for the first time—found guilty of biting an opponent.

But he always scored a lot of goals, and in January 2011, Kenny Dalglish, the Liverpool manager, spotted his genius and brought him to England. There was no shortage of either goals or trouble at Liverpool. In fall 2011 Suárez got banned for racial slurs against Manchester United's fullback, Patrice Evra, and in spring 2013 he got banned again for biting Chelsea's Branislav Ivanović. Suárez was also regularly accused of diving to get penalties.

Suárez shaped up considerably, and during the 2013–2014 season he established himself as one of the world's top goal scorers. He could score tap-ins and long-range goals, dribble past defenders and put the ball in the back of the net, and score with headers. Basically, Suárez could do anything and everything.

But as always, Suárez was his own worst enemy. In Brazil's 2014 World Cup, he bit an opponent for the third time! This time the victim was Italy's Giorgio Chiellini. Suárez was suspended for nine international matches, fined $119,000, and banned from entering any soccer stadium for four months.

Liverpool finally gave up on him and allowed him to leave for Barcelona, which was his dream. Buying this troublemaker was considered a high-risk move for Barça, but Suárez has stayed out of trouble. Playing alongside Messi and (at first) Neymar has allowed his genius to flourish. Suárez scored 59 goals in 53 games during the 2015–2016 season.

SUÁREZ

Suárez was born in the small town of Salto, Uruguay, just like his contemporary Edinson Cavani. Growing up, they never knew each other.

URUGUAY

LUIS SUÁREZ
STRIKER
URUGUAY

HEIGHT 6'
BORN JANUARY 24, 1987
IN SALTO, URUGUAY
CURRENT TEAM:
BARCELONA, SPAIN
INTERNATIONAL GAMES: 97
GOALS: 50